NAVAJO CODE TALKERS

BY EMILY SCHLESINGER

WH/TE L/GHTNING

B O O K S®

N O N F I C T I O N

SADDLEBACK
EDUCATIONAL PUBLISHING
www.sdlback.com

Photo credits: pages 4/5: Historical / Corbis Historical via Getty Images; pages 6/7: Interim Archives / Archive Photos via Getty Images; page 11: Three Lions / Hulton Archive via Getty Images; page 13: Hulton Archive / Archive Photos via Getty Images; pages 14/15: USMC / Hulton Archive via Getty Images; pages 20/21: Interim Archives / Archive Photos via Getty Images; pages 22/23: Fox Photos / Hulton Archive via Getty Images; pages 26/27: PhotoQuest / Archive Photos via Getty Images; page 28: Everett Collection / Shutterstock.com; page 39: Culture Club / Hulton Archive via Getty Images; pages 40/41: Bert Soibelman / Archive Photos via Getty Images; page 45: Rosemarie Mosteller / Shutterstock.com; pages 46/47: Hulton Archive / Archive Photos via Getty Images; page 49: Sean Pavone / Dreamstime.com; pages 50/51: Keystone / Hulton Archive via Getty Images; pages 50/51: Interim Archives / Archive Photos via Getty Images; page 51: Interim Archives / Archive Photos via Getty Images; page 53: National Archives / Hulton Archive via Getty Images; pages 54/55: FPG / Archive Photos via Getty Images; pages 56/57: Mario Tama / Getty Images News via Getty Images

ISBN: 978-1-68021-884-8
eBook: 978-1-64598-208-1

Printed in Malaysia

25 24 23 22 21   1 2 3 4 5

Table of Contents

Unbreakable

U.S. Marines had just landed on a tiny island. The unit was in big trouble. Japanese forces were firing at them. Troops needed help fast. The leader gave an order. One of his soldiers sent an **urgent** message by radio. It sounded like this.

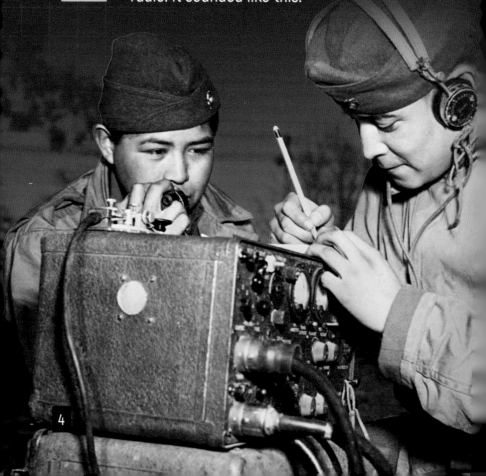

"*Dibeh ah-na a-chin be*
Ah-deel-tahi
D-ah na-as-tso-si
Than-zie tlo-chin
Lin dot-sahi
Tka ha-sta na-kih shush."

Another man sat on a beach nearby. The message came in on his radio. He **translated** the words in his head.

"Sheep eyes nose deer
Demolition
Tea mouse
Turkey onion
Sick horse
Three six two bear."

The man knew exactly what this meant. He scribbled it down fast. *Send demolition team to hill 362B.*

On the front line, the leader paced. Soon he saw help coming. Flame tanks rolled in. A demolition team took over. They saved the lives of the men under fire.

This was World War II. Fighting raged across the globe. Lives hung in the balance. But a top-secret program had been formed. It involved an unbreakable **code**.

FAST FACT: A flame tank has a flamethrower attached to it. These could shoot fire at enemies up to 120 yards away.

A group of men worked behind the scenes. Others did not know what they did. Their work saved thousands of lives. But this secret stayed buried for decades.

Keeping Secrets

Conflict ripped nations apart. Bombs rained over Europe. There was fighting in Asia. World War II had begun.

The U.S. did not want to get involved. But it could not stay out forever. On December 7, 1941, Japanese planes bombed an American base. This was at Pearl Harbor in Hawaii. The next day, the U.S. declared war on Japan.

America was not fully ready for war. Supplies had to be built up. More soldiers were needed. Something else was missing too. Troops did not have a good way to communicate.

Events Leading Up to the Attack at Pearl Harbor

1931

SEPTEMBER
Japan invades China

1939

SEPTEMBER
Germany begins invading neighboring countries

Great Britain and France declare war on Germany, beginning World War II

1941

AUGUST
U.S. cuts off oil supplies to Japan, leaving Japan short of fuel

DECEMBER
Japan attacks the U.S. at Pearl Harbor

1933

MARCH
Adolf Hitler comes to power in Germany

1940

SEPTEMBER
Japan invades Indochina (Southeast Asia)

Japan joins pact with Germany and Italy to form Axis Powers

U.S. begins sending aid and supplies to help China and the Allied Powers in Europe

1930 - 1939

1940 - 1949

Today it's easy to send fast messages. This was not true back then. There were only a few ways. Telephone was one. Radio was another. Both could be tapped. Others could listen in.

This was a big problem. What if enemies heard military messages? It could put troops in danger.

The Need for Codes

Armies have tried to solve this problem. They used codes. These are a way to keep messages secret.

Codes were used during the American Revolution in the 1700s. George Washington's men had several. One was the Culper Code. It used numbers in place of words. Some messages were sent in invisible ink. A message could be held near a flame. Then the ink would change color.

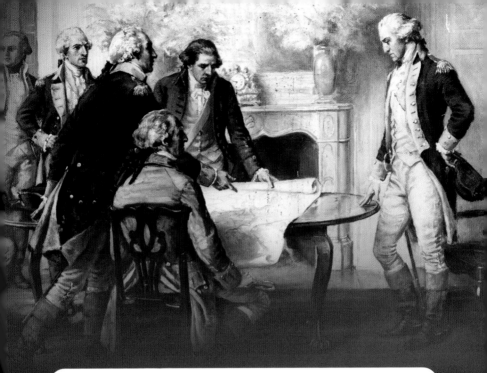

CAESAR'S CODE

Julius Caesar's ancient Roman army used a simple code to communicate. It's called a shift code. In this type of code, each letter in the alphabet shifts over a certain number of places. Suppose the shift is two. *A* becomes *C*. *B* turns to *D*. *C* is *E*.

SHIFT
2
→

A B C D E F G H I J K L

↓ ↓ ↓

A B C D E F G H I J K L M N

"CAESAR'S CODE" would be written "ECGUCT'U EQFG."

Most codes had problems. Simple ones were quick to read. They were also easy to crack. Complex codes were harder to figure out. But they took much longer to read. Messages were often urgent. Troops needed to respond quickly. Complicated codes made this more difficult.

There was another issue. Many codes required a code book. This was a key. It could fall into enemy hands.

THE ENIGMA MACHINE

Machines could produce complex codes. The Germans used one during World War II. It was called Enigma. Its code had over 158 quintillion possible solutions. The Germans thought no one could break it. But Polish agents found an Enigma for sale at a trade fair. The Allies used it to read German messages.

Language as Code

It was World War I. U.S. leaders had an idea. There were hundreds of Native American **tribes**. Many spoke their own **languages**. Few outsiders could understand them. These languages could be used as codes.

There was a problem after the war. Germany and Japan sent spies to the U.S. These spies visited tribes. They learned important words. It could have been enough to break the codes. The U.S. needed a new plan fast.

The Navajo Answer

It was 1942. Philip Johnston was reading the news. A story caught his eye. There was an Army unit in Louisiana. They were trying to come up with a code. It had to be one the Japanese could not break. Johnston's eyes lit up. He knew what would work.

An Unusual Childhood

Johnston's parents were missionaries. When he was young, they moved to a reservation. This was Native American land. It was mostly in Arizona. The tribe that lived there was the Navajo.

His family was white. But Johnston played with kids in the tribe. They spoke Navajo. Johnston learned it too. Soon he knew it well.

Later, Johnston fought in World War I. Codes were used in that war. Years passed. Then he saw the article. Johnston rushed to a naval office. He set up a meeting with Major James E. Jones.

Johnston explained his idea. They should use the Navajo language. It would make the best code. Then he said why.

Why Navajo?

Many Native American languages were related.
People could study one. This helped them
understand others.

Navajo was different. The sounds were unusual.
People used four **pitches**. These changed the
meaning of a word. Children grew up hearing the
sounds. They could understand them. It was hard
for adults to learn, though.

The **grammar** was difficult too. A word could have up to ten prefixes. These might change the meaning of a whole sentence.

FAST FACT: There are over 30 ways to pronounce the word *wind* in Navajo. Each pronunciation gives the word a slightly different meaning.

People could not study Navajo in books. The language was not written. It was only spoken.

The Germans had never learned Navajo. Japanese soldiers did not know it either. Using it as a code seemed like a good idea. U.S. military leaders wanted to test it.

A few Navajo were invited in. They went to two rooms. Each had a phone in it. The men spoke into these. One man was given a message. "Dive bomber attack at dawn." He said it in Navajo. Another man listened. He translated it to English. This was done several times.

Some worried the translations would be off. They were not. Each one was perfect. The military was impressed. They began to **recruit** Navajo soldiers.

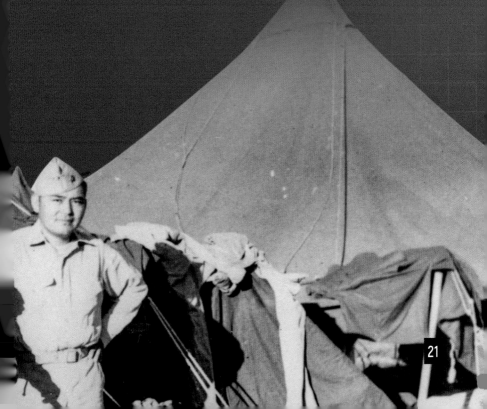

From Reservation to War

Keith Little was a Navajo teen. He attended a boarding school. Ganado Mission was its name. This was in Arizona.

Students were having a picnic. One noticed salt was missing. He ran in the building to get it. When he came back, his face looked strange. The boy said the U.S. had been attacked. Pearl Harbor was bombed.

The class gathered around a radio. President Franklin D. Roosevelt was on the air. He said it was a "date which will live in **infamy**." The U.S. and Japan were at war.

At the school, posters started appearing. They showed Marines. There was a message. It said these were the best soldiers in the world. Little wanted to be one of them. Soon he turned 17. He **enlisted**.

Finding the Right Fit

Peter MacDonald was another Navajo boy. He grew up near the Four Corners. This is where four states meet. They are Arizona, Utah, Colorado, and New Mexico.

MacDonald went to Shiprock Boarding School. He dropped out after sixth grade. Then he trained to be a medicine man. But MacDonald did not want to do that either.

There was a trading post nearby. People came from all over to sell goods. Teens started showing up in sharp blue uniforms. They had joined the Marines. MacDonald was curious. He liked the suits. Soon he joined too.

A Tradition of Service

The Navajo have their own government. It is called the Navajo Nation. They follow U.S. rules as well.

Some U.S. policies have harmed them. One time was in the 1860s. Many were forced to leave their homes. Hundreds died on the journey. Another bad time was in the 1930s. The government killed many of their animals. They said the animals were harming the soil.

The Navajo never forgot. Still, they wanted to serve their country. The U.S. was their homeland. They would defend it. Large numbers **volunteered** after Pearl Harbor.

FAST FACT: Over 44,000 Native Americans served in World War II. This was more than ten percent of their population. Today, Native Americans serve in the military at a higher rate than any other group.

Chester Nez enlisted. He explained why. "A warrior is someone who cares for and protects the people he loves and the land he loves. It was my country that was attacked by the Japanese. I had no choice. I had to join the Marines. I had to be a warrior."

CHESTER NEZ

A Secret Project

Chester Nez was puzzled. Basic training had ended. The other soldiers went home for vacation. But he was not allowed to go. Instead, they moved him to a new base. He was led into a strange building.

The door opened. Nez was surprised by what he saw. There were dozens of men. Almost all were Navajo like him.

CHESTER NEZ

The Assignment

A major got up. He began to talk. This was a top-secret project, he said. The men would create a code. It would use their own language. Then he left. Guards locked the door. They surrounded the building. No one could go in or out.

Military staff were there. They held up pictures. Some showed fighter jets. Others showed weapons. There were all kinds of ships. These were terms that would be used often. The code would have to include them.

The men studied the pictures. There was a problem. The Navajo did not have words for any of these machines.

They thought for a bit. Each picture reminded them of something. One showed a tank. It was covered in armor. Tanks moved slowly too. This reminded them of a turtle. They called it a *chay-da-gahi*. That means "tortoise" in Navajo.

Next they saw a fighter plane. It was small and fast. This made them think of a tiny bird. They named it a *da-he-tih-hi*. That means "hummingbird."

A submarine was next. This moved underwater. It looked like a fish. But it was made of metal. They called it an "iron fish." The Navajo word is *besh-lo*.

The team went on and on. They used their imaginations. The list got long. Soon they had a dictionary. A code was taking shape.

Code Word Examples

TERM	CODE WORD IN ENGLISH	CODE WORD IN NAVAJO
battleship	whale	*lo-tso*
bomb	egg	*a-ye-shi*
bomber plane	buzzard	*jay-sho*
destroyer	shark	*ca-lo*
dive bomber	chicken hawk	*gini*
fighter jet	hummingbird	*da-he-tih-hi*
grenade	potato	*ni-ma-si*
mine sweeper	beaver	*cha*
submarine	iron fish	*besh-lo*
tank	tortoise	*chay-da-gahi*

The Alphabet Code

The men made up words for every machine of war. They had words for commanders and other ranks. Common words also received codes. *When* was "weasel hen." *That* was "turkey hat."

Not every word could have a code. That would be too much. The group added a second type of code. This could spell out words.

They took each letter of the alphabet. First, the men thought of an English word. For example, they chose "ant" for *A*. They picked "bear" for *B*. *C* was "cat." *D* was "deer."

PUTTING TOGETHER MESSAGES

The code talkers formed sentences by using a mix of code words and alphabet letters. For example, the message "Send tank" was made by spelling out *send* and using the code word for *tank*.

English	sheep (S)	eyes (E)	nose (N)	deer (D)	+ tortoise (TANK)
Navajo	*dibeh*	*ah-nah*	*a-chin*	*be*	*chay-da-gahi*

Dibeh ah-nah a-chin be chay-da-gahi means "SEND TANK."

Next, they translated each word into Navajo. "Ant" is *wol-la-chee*. "Bear" is *shush*. "Cat" is *moasi*. "Deer" is *be*. In this way, they could spell out words. *Shush wol-la-chee be* spelled "bad."

Still, experts worried the code could be cracked. Some letters repeated often. This could give clues. The group came up with a solution. More code words were added for each letter. For example, *A* was "ant." They added "apple" and "axe." When *A* was needed, any of these words could be used. These made the code harder.

It was time to test the new code. A code talker was given a message. He said it in code. The listener had to **decipher** it. Then he said its meaning in English. With another code, this might have taken hours. But the Navajo did it in two and a half minutes. The code worked.

Sample Alphabet Code

LETTER	CODE WORD IN ENGLISH	CODE WORD IN NAVAJO
A	ant	*wol-la-chee*
B	badger	*na-hash-chid*
C	cat	*moasi*
D	deer	*be*
E	ear	*ah-jah*
F	fir	*chuo*
G	girl	*ah-tad*
H	hair	*tse-gah*
I	ice	*tkin*
J	jaw	*ah-ya-tsinne*
K	kettle	*jad-ho-loni*
L	lamb	*dibeh-yazzie*
M	match	*tsin-tliti*
N	needle	*tsah*
O	oil	*a-kha*
P	pant	*cla-gi-aih*
Q	quiver	*ca-yeilth*
R	rabbit	*gah*
S	sheep	*dibeh*
T	tea	*d-ah*
U	uncle	*shi-da*
V	victor	*a-keh-di-glini*
W	weasel	*gloe-ih*
X	cross	*al-na-as-dzoh*
Y	yucca	*tsah-as-zih*
Z	zinc	*besh-do-tliz*

Code in Action

It was August 1942. The code talkers were sent to Guadalcanal. They began their first mission. This was with the First Marine Division.

The men were being tested. Their code had worked back home. Could they perform under the stress of battle?

FAST FACT: Guadalcanal is the largest of the Solomon Islands. It is located in the South Pacific.

Under Fire

Chester Nez remembered the awful sounds. They lasted day and night. Shells exploded. Machine guns fired. Bombs dropped. There was hand-to-hand fighting.

Nez was also afraid of the crocodiles. The jungle was full of them. They came out at night.

Still, he did his job. He remembered the first message he sent. This was during combat. It read like this. "Enemy machine gun nest on your right flank. Destroy."

SOLOMON ISLANDS

Guadalcanal

Nez worked with a partner. They used a TBX radio. It was the size of a toolbox. The two took turns. One spun a crank to power the radio. The other spoke into a microphone. This was how messages were sent.

They had no code book. That would be too risky. The enemy could get it. Everything had to be done by memory.

General Vandegrift was in charge of the code talkers. He watched them for weeks. Soon he had seen enough. He sent a message back to the U.S. "This Navajo code is terrific. The enemy never understood it. We don't understand it either. But it works. Send us some more Navajos."

STORIES AND MEMORY

The Navajo code grew to include hundreds of words. This would be hard for most people to remember. But the Navajo had an advantage. Their language was not written. Stories were passed down orally. Children started memorizing them from the age of three. They had to get every word right. Only then could they "graduate" to the next story.

Risk

Hundreds more Navajo were recruited. These code talkers were sent to islands across the Pacific. The men went to places like Tinian and Tarawa. They landed at Guadalcanal and Guam.

Code talkers worked on the front lines. They faced many dangers. It was not just the fighting. There were also threats from within.

FAST FACT: The Navajo were not the only code talkers. Small numbers of Chippewa, Comanche, Hopi, and other tribes also served as code talkers during World War II.

Mistaken Identity

The code talkers' jobs were top secret. Enemy soldiers could not find out. U.S. troops could not know either. That was too big a risk. Their secret could get out.

Fellow soldiers would wonder about them. Who were these men? What did they do? The Navajo looked different from them too. Some were mistaken for Japanese soldiers.

Samuel Tom Holiday was a code talker. He was hiking. The area was muddy. Then he saw something. It was a pair of Japanese shoes. Holiday had an idea. His own boots were covered in mud. He put on the shoes. Next he cleaned his boots.

It happened fast. Marines jumped on him. His gun was ripped away. Then someone recognized him. The men saw their mistake. "Get those things off your feet!" they said.

Another time, Holiday had taken off his uniform. He felt something touch his back. It was a **bayonet**. A Marine forced him to walk. Holiday was locked up with Japanese prisoners. Later, someone from his team saw him there. Only then was he freed.

Protection

These mix-ups happened often. The military tried something new. They gave each code talker a **bodyguard**.

The two went everywhere together. They shared a **foxhole**. One would sleep. The other kept watch. Now the code talkers were safer. These men formed loyal bonds.

There was a dark side too. Rumors went around. Bodyguards had a special order. A code talker might get captured. Then his bodyguard would have to shoot him. The code could not fall into enemy hands. Luckily, this never happened.

CAPTURE

Being captured was a big risk. The Japanese targeted radiomen. Code talkers had to move from place to place to avoid being caught. One time a Navajo man was captured. The Japanese interrogated him. He refused to translate a message. It turned out he was not a code talker. The man understood the words. But he did not know what the sentence meant. The code stayed safe throughout the war.

Winning the Pacific

The U.S. had a strategy. It would destroy Japanese bases. Many were on islands. This was known as "island-hopping."

Marines landed on shore. Code talkers went too. Some sent secret orders. Others gave warnings. Their words launched attacks. They kept units safe. Battles were won this way.

Iwo Jima

One of the biggest battles was on Iwo Jima. The U.S. wanted to take this island. They would use it as a base. It was flying distance to the mainland. This made it perfect for **air raids**.

FAST FACT: Iwo Jima is a Japanese island south of Tokyo, Japan. It is only eight square miles in size.

Marines arrived at the island. It was February 19, 1945. All seemed peaceful. The U.S. thought they could take it easily. But 18,000 Japanese troops were hiding. They began to fire. This was a surprise. Many Americans died.

Others pressed on. They made it a few yards at a time. It took days to reach the top of the island. There, they planted an American flag. News was sent back to the U.S. The message was in Navajo.

RAISING THE FLAG ON IWO JIMA

A photographer snapped a picture on Iwo Jima. It showed six Marines putting up an American flag. This became one of the most famous images of World War II. A sculpture based on this image is displayed at the Marine Corps War Memorial in Washington, D.C.

Fighting continued. Japanese soldiers took cover in caves. Others were **camouflaged** in jungles. U.S. planes dropped bombs. But the Japanese were safely hidden. They continued to fight back.

Troops had to stay alert. Communication had to be fast. They depended on the code talkers. Two days were especially important. Code talkers worked nonstop during this time. Over 800 messages were sent. Not one had a mistake.

The bloodshed went on for a month. Then Marines found the last holdouts. They hid in a valley. It was called Bloody Gorge. For ten days, the two sides fought hard. Finally, the Japanese lost. The U.S. took the island.

A Turning Point

Iwo Jima was one of the toughest battles in the war. The code talkers helped win it. This was a **turning point** for the U.S. They put the island to use. Planes landed there in emergencies. This saved 24,000 lives. It also helped the **Allies** capture Okinawa.

Major Howard Connor was in charge of communications. He saw everything that happened. His opinion was clear. "Were it not for the Navajos, the Marines would never have taken Iwo Jima," he said.

THE END OF THE WAR

In May 1945, Germany surrendered to the Allies in Europe. But Japan kept fighting. More than 12,000 Americans were killed while invading Okinawa. Thousands more would die if the fighting continued. Instead, the U.S. dropped the world's first atomic bomb on Hiroshima. A second was dropped on Nagasaki. Both Japanese cities were destroyed. Japan surrendered. World War II ended in September of 1945.

Returning Home

World War II ended on September 2, 1945.
The code talkers should have been
welcomed home as heroes. But their work
had to remain secret. This was an order.
What if the code was needed again?

Friends and family asked about the war. The code
talkers said little. This was not easy. They had been
highly respected. Their work saved lives. Now it was
like nothing had happened.

Finding jobs was difficult too. Code talkers learned valuable skills. They could not tell employers this. Some had to take low-skill work.

The code talkers had learned their own value, however. They knew what they were capable of. This inspired them to aim high. Some went to college. Others started businesses. Many became leaders in their communities.

The End of the Secret

The code talkers kept their secret for over 20 years. This ended in 1968. The U.S. made a decision. It would **declassify** the code talker program.

Now these men could speak the truth. First they told their families. Then they told friends. It took time for the public to understand.

Recognition

Many years passed. It was 1982. The code talkers were invited to Washington, D.C. President Reagan gave them an award. He made August 14 a national holiday. It became Navajo Code Talkers Day.

In 2000, the men were invited back. This time they received the Congressional Gold Medal.

The following years brought fame at last. Hollywood made a movie about the code talkers. It was called *Windtalkers*. Many books came out too. They told what the men did. A few were best sellers.

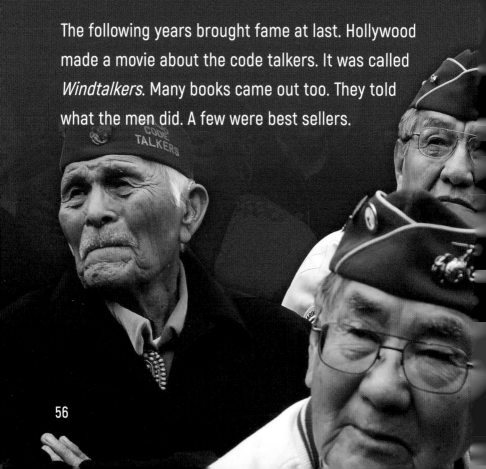

Remembering the Code Talkers

There were once over 400 Navajo code talkers. Only a few are still alive. The group may be small. But they have big plans. One is to build a new museum. It will honor the code talkers. Future generations will learn their story.

The Navajo did what seemed impossible. They came up with an unbreakable code. For years, their silence was unbroken too.

Now their work is a mystery no more. It helped win the war. The code talkers are heroes.

Glossary

air raid: an attack in which planes drop bombs

Allies: the countries that fought against Germany in World War II

bayonet: a sharp knife at the end of a rifle

bodyguard: a person who travels with someone to protect them from harm

camouflage: a way to hide by blending into the surroundings

code: a system of letters, sounds, or symbols used in place of normal words to send messages

decipher: to find the meaning of a code

declassify: to release information that was once kept secret

enlist: to join the military

foxhole: an underground hiding place used to keep safe from enemy fire

grammar: rules that determine how words are used in a language

infamy: the state of being well known due to bad or evil deeds

language: words, symbols, or signs used to communicate

pitch: how high or low a sound is

recruit: to get people to join the military

translate: to turn words from one language into another

tribe: a group of people with strong cultural or family bonds

turning point: a moment when an important change takes place

urgent: extremely important; needing immediate attention

volunteer: to offer services without the expectation of payment

CHILDREN
OF THE
HOLOCAUST

CHAPTER
2

A Deadly
Idea

Six million Jewish people were killed in the **Holocaust**. They had not done anything wrong. These people lost their lives for being Jewish. It was a **genocide**.

The events leading up to this started in Germany. A new political party had come to power. It was the Nazi Party. Adolf Hitler was their leader. He became **chancellor** in 1933.

DEMOCRACY TO DICTATORSHIP

Germany held an election in 1932. Hitler's Nazi Party won 230 seats in the government. The Communists won the second-largest number of seats. Several months later, there was a fire in the main government building. The Nazis blamed the Communists. They used the fire as an excuse to take over the government. This made Germany a one-party dictatorship.

FAST FACT: The official name of the Nazi Party was the National Socialist German Workers' Party.

8

9

At each stop, Naphtali tried again. He went to five cars. Finally, Lulek answered. Naphtali used a pin to open the door. The brothers raced back under the belly of the train. They climbed into the men's car. Lulek was safe for now.

Soon they arrived at Buchenwald. This was one of the deadliest camps. Naphtali wrapped Lulek in a pillow. He carried him in a sack on his back.

Then Naphtali saw something happening. Prisoners' bags were being thrown into an oven. He yelled at Lulek to get out of his bag.

A German guard spotted the boy. His brother thought fast. Their mom had left him a gold watch. He threw it at the guard. The man let Lulek pass.

A number was assigned to Lulek. It was 117030. Prisoners wore patches too. These were sewn on uniforms. They had shapes and letters. This was how prisoners were **classified**. Lulek's showed he was Jewish. Officers treated Jews the worst.

FAST FACT: Buchenwald did not have gas chambers. Still, many died at the camp. Prisoners starved or got diseases. Others were executed.

NAZI GERMANY

✕ Buchenwald

117030

Kindertransport Routes

Children boarded trains in major cities. These took them to ports in Belgium and the Netherlands. Then ships took them to Harwich, England.

MAP KEY	
————	Train Route 🚂
——	Ship Route ⛴

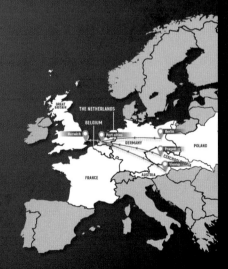

WHITE LIGHTNING BOOKS® NONFICTION

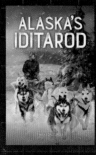
ALASKA'S IDITAROD

CHILDREN OF THE HOLOCAUST

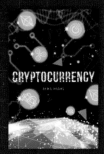
CRYPTOCURRENCY

DEADLY BITES

DIGITAL WORLDS

DROIDS AND ROBOTS

ESPORTS

FLIGHT SQUADS

NAVAJO CODE TALKERS

OLYMPIC GAMES

STEPHEN HAWKING
HIS LIFE AND LEGACY

SUPERBUGS

THE WHITE HOUSE

WORKING DOGS

WORLD CUP SOCCER

MORE TITLES COMING SOON
SDLBACK.COM/WHITE-LIGHTNING-BOOKS